RENDEZVOUS

INTENSE POEMS

APAR SINGH

This collection of poems is dedicated to the energy that I feel. This energy has liberated me, and given new wings to my imagination.

It's an energy due to which art exists in this world, and which every artist searches for. Like my previous ones, this work too is dedicated to the same heavenly energy.

Contents

Foreword

I am wondering what is more,
Your affection or my attraction?
Which of two is a lethal weapon,
Your seduction or my admiration?

--

Nothing like a rendezvous,
A place where lovers meet.
Far from world's prying eyes,
Open up, listen and speak.

--

The soul that I'd rather prefer,
Is caring, generous & selfless.
Sweet love of innocent kids,
Who laugh and cry, hopeless.

Preface

This poetry book gives a expression to my feelings, which are hard to convey in person. It was written almost two months back. Recent times have been very emotionally charged ones, sometimes disorienting, while others reassuring. Writing these poems helped me put my mind at ease, and will resonate with those readers who remember what swimming in love lake is like.

These poems are for those trying to figure out love, or wishing to relive this nerve wrecking experience. I hope you'll find it an iteresting read.

Prologue

I shudder at the thought,
Of coming here sans you.
Who'll meet me downstairs?
I'll badly, madly seek you.
I can't even to imagine,
Carrying on without you.
Who'll meet me downstairs?
I'll sadly, glumly miss you.
I don't know if I'll get thru,
Without your shining light.
Who'll meet me downstairs?
To make it seem all right.
I don't wanna miss a day,
I dig listening, watching you.
Who'll meet me downstairs?
Without thee, will go askew.
I don't know anything here,
Without you it's a nightmare.
Who'll meet me downstairs?
I'd skip it, if you aren't there.

1. Lover

Who is a lover? I looked it up on internet and it says a partner in a sexual or romantic relationship. They make distinctions beteen a lover, a boyfriend, a soulmate and a husband. They say lovers are in for the short-term. They say lovers are non-commital.

In this world of clear disctinctions and moral policing, they don't talk about the possibility of a lover being a boyfriend, a soulmate and a partner. Does it always have to follow the same order of progression? The orders of a crumbling and dying system.

Rendezvous

Nothing like a rendezvous,
A place where lovers meet.
Far from world's prying eyes,
Open up, listen and speak.

Feels tender, yet so strong,
A proclivity for staying long.
Precious meets, try to prolong,
Fondness and warmth's song.

Tryst with the special one,
A stamping ground like none.
At the haunt every time re-run,
Going around often, for its fun.

Where does it leads one to?
I believe another rendezvous.
On your heart I plan a coup,
All unmet desires made anew.

Gait

Know when you're around,
Have picked up your gait.
Know where to seek you,
Everyday imbibe your trait.

Even in the dreams at night,
You're one I hang out with.
With you I shine bright,
Divine brilliance, no myth.

These feels reek of mystery,
Unspoken, peculiar history.
Never seen sparks so adrift,
The air reeks of chemistry.

I live by your zest and laughter,
Keep harbouring the fuel of life.
Hold me closer to you forever,
I'm on standby, keep at bay trife.

Every day

I hope to see you every day,
Some days barely get through.
Looking to find us some time,
Somehow making it through.

I'm slow, you make me bold,
My desire's to take your hold.
If only the truth shall be told,
You've fixed my broken mould.

I wish to peek into your heart,
Seeking to discover some love.
Can't make out, trying to flirt,
Thinking of you lying in alcove.

I am wondering what is more,
Your affection or my attraction?
Which of two is a lethal weapon,
Your seduction or my admiration?

Fervour

I tend to stray without you,
You make this life bearable.
Keep you close to my heart,
The distances feel terrible.

I can't seem to think straight,
Unjust is my unending wait.
Don't think I ask for too much,
Let me thru your heart's gate.

Often I tend to lose patience,
My chest's under this weight.
Guess not been good enough,
To forever keep you, my mate.

You're my guide, shining light,
With a fervor burning so bright.
Only one who's worth a fight,
Won't ever let go, hold me tight.

Resurrection

I learnt to see, walk ahead,
Following and pursuing you.
I could never give, forgive,
Swapped my world view.

I'm standing one call away,
Your wish is my command.
Over me you do hold sway,
Spellbound by a magic wand.

Neither can fake chemistry,
Nor can impel an attraction.
Felicity of karmic serendipity,
Make love to me, resurrection.

Its likely I've found after all,
One I've been looking for.
A friend, ally, comrade, love,
Worthy to keep struggling for.

Floy

This face makes heart dove,
It's the golden heart I vie for.
There's so much left to love,
Each facet's worth fighting for.

You've always brought me joy,
I eat, sleep and feel content.
All my desires and wishes floy,
Our time together's well spent.

Even if don't get enough sleep,
I still wake up feeling relaxed.
Like you're always by my side,
World's best feeling I ever had.

You know the arts of seduction,
Bland life's pleasant exception.
Every time make right moves,
Music on a verge of perfection.

Tell me what's unsettling you,
For nothing I'd spare to gratify.
We mustn't let one other down,

What lacks, our union'll satisfy.

Forever

We are believers in forever,
Why can't we love again?
Always had it for one other,
Let the love games begin.

Never had a dull moment,
Even if we've made a fuss.
Vibes beyond the firmament,
Go easy, why miss the bus?

Time's been vanished in trough,
In lands and people unknown.
Hope wouldn't have been tough,
Living apart, feels outgrown?

After long found one another,
Feel free to reach me, whenever.
Let's make the most of time,
And embark on this endeavour.

Tamed

A girl's desire to be tamed,
A secret unknown to men.
Always hidden in plain sight,
A mill wherein desires bran.

Try to read between the lines,
Do what needs to be done.
Glance, kiss, touch and hold her,
Passions make her fabric undone.

Either you shall blitzkrieg her,
Or perpetually stand in queue.
Treat her as the special one,
Unleashing true colors and hue.

Don't mess up by going askew,
Turning lento making her brew.
Just get it off and give her due,
Babes just want you to subdue.

Hooked

I am hooked to your eyes,
On me why not take a bet?
I am crazy for you voice,
Try me now than later regret.

I am hooked to your smile,
Distraction and uneasiness.
I move from nadir to zenith,
In a matter of few moments.

I am hooked to your thoughts,
Missing you tears me asunder.
I am not myself without you,
Being awkward and a blunder.

I am hooked to unhook you,
How to keep desires dormant?
I have always vied for you,
This separation is a torment.

I am hooked like a addict,
It's too late to let go of now.
I just wanna see you more,

Want to meet you anyhow.

Hankering

Days are endless, far too long,
Nights needlessly prolong.
All sans you, a waste of time,
In Inamorata's arms I belong.

There's a spark in your voice,
A hidden mystery in your eyes.
Hankering of an itchy misfit,
Kills me to see you blink twice.

You're the only flower I smell,
Tending to you is my pleasure.
All adages falling short of you,
Each moment is a rare treasure.

You're too far from the eye,
I've turned brazen and gruff.
I'm intent, keep giving it a try,
Less of you's making it tough.

It's time a caterpillar must die,
Cocoon shall birth a butterfly.
Don't care how hard the shell,

Gonna give it all I have, and fly.

Love

If our soul's a kinda vessel,
How much can it ever hold?
You feel there're your mate,
How surely it be really told?

The soul that I'd rather prefer,
Is caring, generous & selfless.
Sweet love of innocent kids,
Who laugh and cry, hopeless.

The love that I'd rather have,
Is young, blissful & timeless.
Salty love of rhyming souls,
It's dorky, fun and limitless.

The warmth I'd rather have,
Is snug, heavenly & limitless.
True love of courting swans,
That's true & fair, ceaseless.

The belle that I'd rather have,
Is alive, charmer & hotness.
The passionate love of Eros,

Ardour & devotion, Lustrous.

Stay

I've been around peeps,
Yet always been alone.
To notions of this world,
Respect I lack, I disown.

Lost in a world of my own,
Haven't I strayed too far?
Fear, sleep, hunger & thirst,
Lost in my drinks that scar.

You've altered this vain life,
We're still afar, yearning.
As I look to end my strife,
Your warm arms, comforting.

Coming from different lives,
Having moved too far away.
Invisible strings bind together,
All I need is for you to stay.

Soon you'll leave me alone,
What'll be left in this life?
Nothing I've coveted more,

Unget-at-able music, arid fife.

In you found my last hope,
A last wish that I've made.
An urge, an utmost desire,
Without you I shall break.

Rise & Fall

Maybe it's to rise back up.
Firstly, we will have to fall,
Like the wind goes absent,
As the heavy storms crawl.

Before I can find real self,
To special one I give it all.
Like the water evaporates,
Then comes back as rainfall.

At times feels like I'm done,
Though I'm still standing tall.
It seems there's a lot to come,
Many a times hitting the wall.

There's always hope to grow,
If the right one could show.
Lovers like kids need to learn,
Until they find the right one.

Every time I wait for her call,
My crazy pulse rises and fall.
She's like a code to decipher,

Wondering if can crack it at all.

Yet

I hate these weak-days,
Yet, look forward to them.
I hate these traffic jams,
Yet, ain't bothered by xem.

I'm indifferent to romance,
Yet, at you I often glance.
I prefer not to take chance,
Yet, for you I'll take a lance.

I'd given up on believing,
Yet, paddling to keep float.
I've hidden long from light,
Yet, setting sail of my boat.

I felt my emotions weaning,
Yet, I long infinitely for you.
I had long ceased dreaming,
Yet, finding my future in you.

I've been detached for aye,
Yet, getting attached to you.
I've longed forever for change,

Yet, I wish to stay on with you.

How else?

Don’t regret a moment of it,
How else we could’ve met?
Won’t push reset button,
Hope’s revived, can’t abet.

Never regret making a bet,
How else we’d have cette?
Won’t push preset button,
Life’s revived, love’s in net.

Won’t regret trying roulette,
How else have a tête-à-tête?
Unpressed the mute button.
Faith’s renewed, my colette.

Shan’t regret making a gamble,
How else our appetites whet?
Go ahead, push select button,
Caret’s gone, found my odette.

Dare not regret taking a chance,
How else could met my life yet?
Don’t bother with back button,

See the rains, break a sweat.

Cold

It's freezing cold outside,
Window panes drops dot.
It's freezing cold inside,
Thine pics melt my heart.

I wake up with a dream,
But where's my strength?
Swim against the stream,
Can to go to any length.

I wake up with desires tall,
Of meeting you, undoable.
Always waiting for your call,
You turn cold, unreachable.

I wake up with your wish,
For day to be unlike previous.
A kiss, more than a squish,
Hope you aren't too oblivious.

I wake up to my last hope,
Can only see obstacles galore.
You kind of feel like a dope,

This isn't fancy, but a lot more.

I wake up to harsh realities,
Am I'm asking for too much?
Wonder what I mean to you,
I'm in it forever, get a hunch.

Wonder

Where did I wanna be?
With you, under the stars.
And I ended up nowhere,
Living with brutal scars.

What I fiercely wanted?
Us, affection, inseparables.
I instead got a elusive life,
Flaky, emptiness, setbacks.

What do I come back to?
Despair always, peace never.
Except I truly connect to,
My lover, now & forever.

What does it means to you?
Undefined, secret, jittery.
Wonder why we even talk?
Perplexed, unsure, mystery.

You ever feel the same pull?
I think so, only you could tell,
If chanced upon my bare soul,

You'd fall too, I long back fell.

But

I wanna bask in the sunshine,
But been locked up for a while.
I dig walking under moon light,
But my stars they won't align.

I wish to shower in those rains,
But haven't been out in a while.
I enjoy the breeze on my face,
But keep it covered all the time.

I long for the blooms of spring,
But haven't smelled them awhile.
I hope of taking the long road,
But hold myself back every time.

I prefer for you not to be gone,
But haven't seen you in a while.
I need to talk from dusk till dawn,
But mostly you're lacking in time.

I'm in need your grace and light,
But we've been vying for a while.
I wish to hold you tight all night,

So lets pace it, why stop on a dime?

Self

Been lying to myself,
All through this time.
Been untrue to myself,
Why I myself beguile?

Been damaging self,
Always been so careless.
Been ignoring intuition,
Always been so reckless.

Been mistaken all along,
Even though I knew it.
Been trudging lifelong,
How could I blow it?

Been losing out on time,
Always acting vaguely.
Am I worth your while?
Been thinking lately.

Been feeling winter waters,
Harshest, crispiest & coldest.
Hope I'll believe in myself,

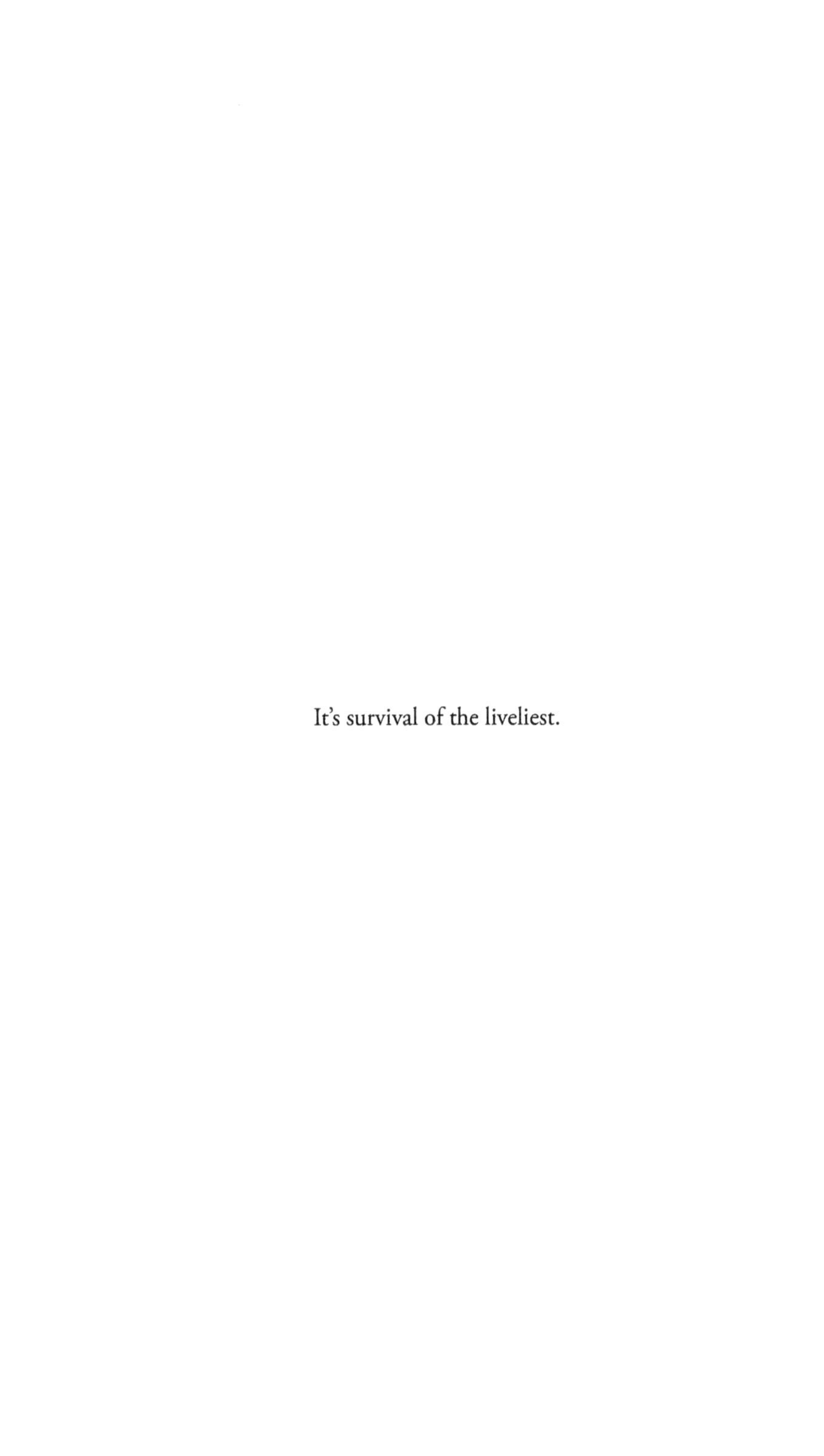

It's survival of the liveliest.

Undone

The bucket list remains undone,
Destinations remain unvisited.
The times of happiness but gone,
Bring strange melancholia instead.

There's nothing I wouldn't do,
To bring those evenings back.
I'll miss your laughter dearly,
But I'm too reluctant to accept.

Your desire, my need & craving,
Brings to me dodgy desperation.
All the time running in my mind,
You'll be my lifetime obsession.

The piercing pain in my heart,
Is possibly more than I can hold.
I'd never wish not make you sad,
My feelings, however must be told.

Now that you're not around me,
I wonder if I've lost my compass.
I'll stay put until you cross me,

You're left, stay in my thoughts.

I am not sure if it's arcanely,
Life's esoteric enmity with thee.
Now that you've left too soon,
And I'll be again an empty me.

9 798886 410341

Printed by Libri Plureos GmbH in Hamburg, Germany